REIHE CANTZ

MATTHEW McCASLIN
AUSSTELLUNGEN EXHIBITIONS

INHALT | CONTENTS

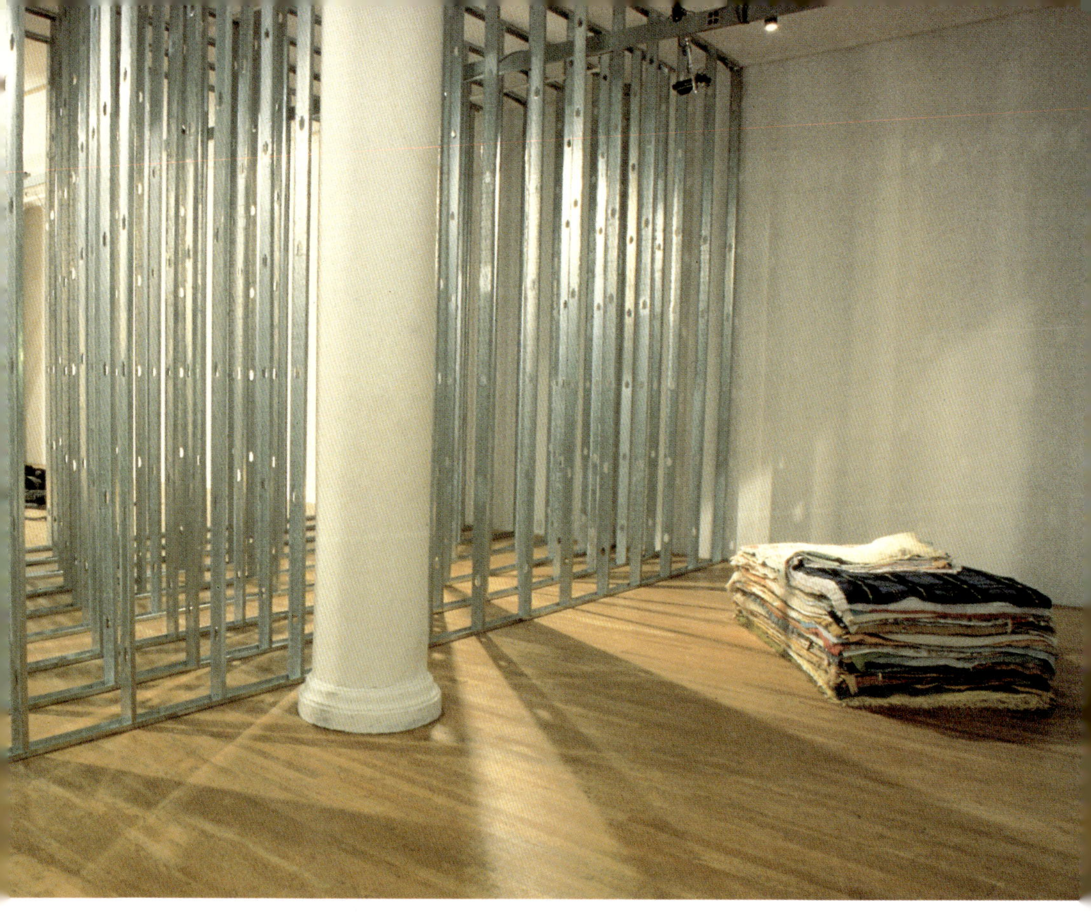

LANDSCAPES OF THE INBETWEEN, DANIEL NEWBURG GALLERY, NEW YORK 1989

NETZWERKE DER KUNST
Die Ausstellungen von Matthew McCaslin

Der Charakter des Transitorischen ist den Installationen von Matthew McCaslin immanent. Die Ausstellungen irritieren zunächst jeden Besucher, der die Präsentationsräume betritt, indem sie die Erwartungen des Kunstpublikums untergraben und es scheinbar mitten in eine Arbeitssituation stellen. McCaslins Installationen simulieren einen Zustand des permanenten Umbruchs. Elektrische Zuleitungen sind kreuz und quer über den Boden gezogen. Ein abgehängtes Deckenelement legt die verborgene Konstruktion der Architektur offen und scheint Teil gerade begonnener Reparaturen zu sein (Abb. S. 14 | 15); ebenso könnte die quer durch den Raum gezogene Rasterstruktur aus Aluminiumstützen auf eine neu einzuziehende Trennwand hinweisen (Abb. S. 6). Über den Fußboden verstreut finden sich zahlreiche abgeschnittene Kabelenden, nicht verwendete Plastikkappen und überzählige Schrauben, als hinterlassene Spuren eines intensiven Arbeitsprozesses.

In seinen Installationen legt Matthew McCaslin die üblicherweise verborgene Infrastruktur der Ausstellungsarchitektur offen, um sie als künstlerischen Werkstoff und mit neuer, ästhetischer Funktion wieder in den Raum einzubringen. Dessen innere Konstruktion aus industriellen Metallgittern und den abgehängten Zwischendecken mit ihrer gesamten elektrischen Versorgung aus Stromkabeln, Lichtschaltern, Mehrfachsteckdosen und offenen Fassungen sind McCaslins Grundmaterialien, die er je nach Bedarf durch Ventilatoren, Uhren und audiovisuelle Geräte erweitert.

Die von Matthew McCaslin für seine Ausstellungen entworfenen Installationen verwandeln den gesamten Raum unter Berücksichtigung seiner spezifischen architektonischen Qualitäten in eine temporäre ästhetische Situation, die nur für wenige Wochen existent bleibt. Die Projekte für die Galerie Jennifer Flay 1991 in Paris (Abb. S. 14 | 15) und das New Yorker Museum of Modern Art im Jahr darauf (Abb. S. 25) waren solche Beispiele. Zugleich ist McCaslin aber auch daran interessiert, über die Arbeit an den Ausstellungen, und zunächst in diese integriert, autonome, nicht ausschließlich an eine Installation gebundene skulpturale Werke zu entwickeln. Sie bilden die über den Raum verteilten künstlerischen Zentren jeder Präsentation, die McCaslin durch ein dicht gespanntes und scheinbar ungeordnetes Durcheinander von Kabeln zu einem interaktiven Netzwerk verbindet. Meist genügt jedoch ein einziger Schalter, um den Energiefluß zu allen Werken zu unterbrechen und die gesamte komplizierte Lichtanlage und Medientechnik lahmzulegen.

Diese Zentren innerhalb der Installationen, in denen McCaslin seine industriellen Materialien zu komplexen Arrangements verdichtet, erhalten damit eine ästhetische Sprengkraft, die ihnen auch über die zeitlich begrenzte Ausstellungssituation eine Existenz als selbständige und mobile plastische Arbeiten sichert. Eher selten hingegen entstehen die Werke im New Yorker Atelier des Künstlers. Dort ist vor allem der Ort für vorbereitende Tätigkeiten, im Laufe derer McCaslin bestimmte Ideen oder Details von Ausstellungskonzeptionen in einer Art Laborsituation simulieren und erproben kann. Konsequent okkupiert er statt dessen die Ausstellungsräume der Galerien und Museen als Ateliers auf Zeit. Nach intensiven Vorarbeiten entstehen hier unter dem Zeitdruck des bevorstehenden Eröffnungstermins die Objekte, die sich mit Hilfe unendlicher Meter von Verlängerungskabeln und unter Einsatz zahlreicher Verbindungsstecker zu einem dichten energetischen Versorgungssystem zusammenschließen.

Bedingt durch diese Arbeitsweise entstehen aus den Ausstellungen heraus Werkgruppen, die durch den Einsatz identischer Materialien und eines verwandten Formenvokabulars gemeinsame Merkmale aufweisen: Scheinbar chaotisch verwickelte und zusammengeschnürte Kabel mit Mehrfachsteckern, zahlreichen Schaltern und verspiegelten Glühlampen charakterisieren beispielsweise die Objekte aus der Präsentation 1992 in der Kölner Galerie Rolf Ricke (Abb. S. 22|23), einfache geometrische Formen beziehungsweise Werkarrangements mit integrierten audio-visuellen Geräten und intensiven Bild-/Tonimpulsen hingegen kennzeichnen die Installationen 1991 (Abb. S. 10|11) und 1993 (Abb. S. 30|31) bei Daniel Newburg in New York.

Nur selten stellt McCaslin seinen Ausstellungen Titel voran. Lediglich für die konzentrierten Objektarrangements, die später auch als selbständige Werke existieren, wählt er ironische und assoziationsreiche Bezeichnungen, wie »48 Hours In A Day«, »Path of Least Resistance« »Revolution« oder »Love Letter«. Häufig leiten sich diese Titel aus der Situation des Herstellungsprozesses her, während sich hinter anderen, eher literarischen Beschreibungen sehr persönliche Geschichten verbergen können.

Mit spielerischer Geste arrangiert McCaslin seine Materialien zu anarchischen Kompositionen, welche die strenge Funktionalität und praktische Effizienz der eingesetzten Standarduhren, Lichtschalter, Verbindungsstecker oder Ventilatoren immer wieder ironisch in Frage stellen. Diese Ästhetik ist von Matthew McCaslins Erfahrungen und seinem Umgang mit den inzwischen historischen künstlerischen Positionen der sechziger Jahre geprägt. Zwei Jahrzehnte später hat er sie wieder aufgegriffen, indem er ihre Formensprache neu definiert, mit aktuellen Themen besetzt und so zu einer eigenständigen Position weiterentwickelt. McCaslins Konzeption trifft sich dabei mit verwandten ästhetischen Entwürfen von anderen Künstlern seiner Generation, wie Matthew Barney, Felix Gonzalez-Torres, Thom Merrick, Cady Noland oder Jessica Stockholder.

Mehrere der charakteristischen Gestaltungsprinzipien postminimalistischer Skulptur kennzeichnen die Werke von Matthew McCaslin. Auch seine Arbeiten zeigen den Verzicht auf präzise strukturierte Kompositionen und lassen statt dessen dem Material Spielraum, so daß Zufall und Chaos den provisorischen Charakter der Installationen prägen. Die Kabelverbindungen, Schalter und Mehrfachsteckdosen stellen dabei nicht nur die Funktionsfähigkeit der Glühlampen, Uhren und Ventilatoren sicher, sondern behaupten sich hier als gleichberechtigtes ästhetisches Material im gestalterischen Prozeß.

Aus der Tradition der frühen Objekte und Installationen von Bruce Nauman oder Keith Sonnier wird auch McCaslins Anspruch verständlich, den Ausstellungsbesucher nicht nur als Betrachter zu fordern, sondern ihn mit möglichst vielfältigen Reizen zu konfrontieren und mehrere seiner Sinne gleichzeitig zu beanspruchen. Dabei steigern gleißend helle Lichtquellen und im schnellen Rhythmus wechselnde Medienbilder die Objekte bereits in ihrer visuellen Präsenz. McCaslin ergänzt sie durch lautstarke akustische Signale, und er läßt für den Ausstellungsbesucher die Kunst durch die von Ventilatoren abgestrahlten Windenergien sogar spürbar werden. Während der Besucher die Installation durchwandert, wird er selbst zum Bestandteil der Ausstellung. Seine Anwesenheit und seine Bewegungen im Raum können das Werk verändern; durch eingebaute Lichtschranken löst er akustische Signale aus, und er kann durch Umlegen eines einzigen Schalters den gesamten Stromkreis der Installation unterbrechen.

Die industriell gefertigten Materialien mit ihrem reduzierten Funktionalismus und den technischen Oberflächen verbinden Matthew McCaslins Werk zwar auch mit der Ästhetik minimalistischer Stilrichtungen. Die Energien, die diese eher statischen Objekte durchströmen, sind jedoch das eigentliche Material in McCaslins Arbeiten, wobei ihr Kreislauf, Austausch und Verlust zum künstleri-

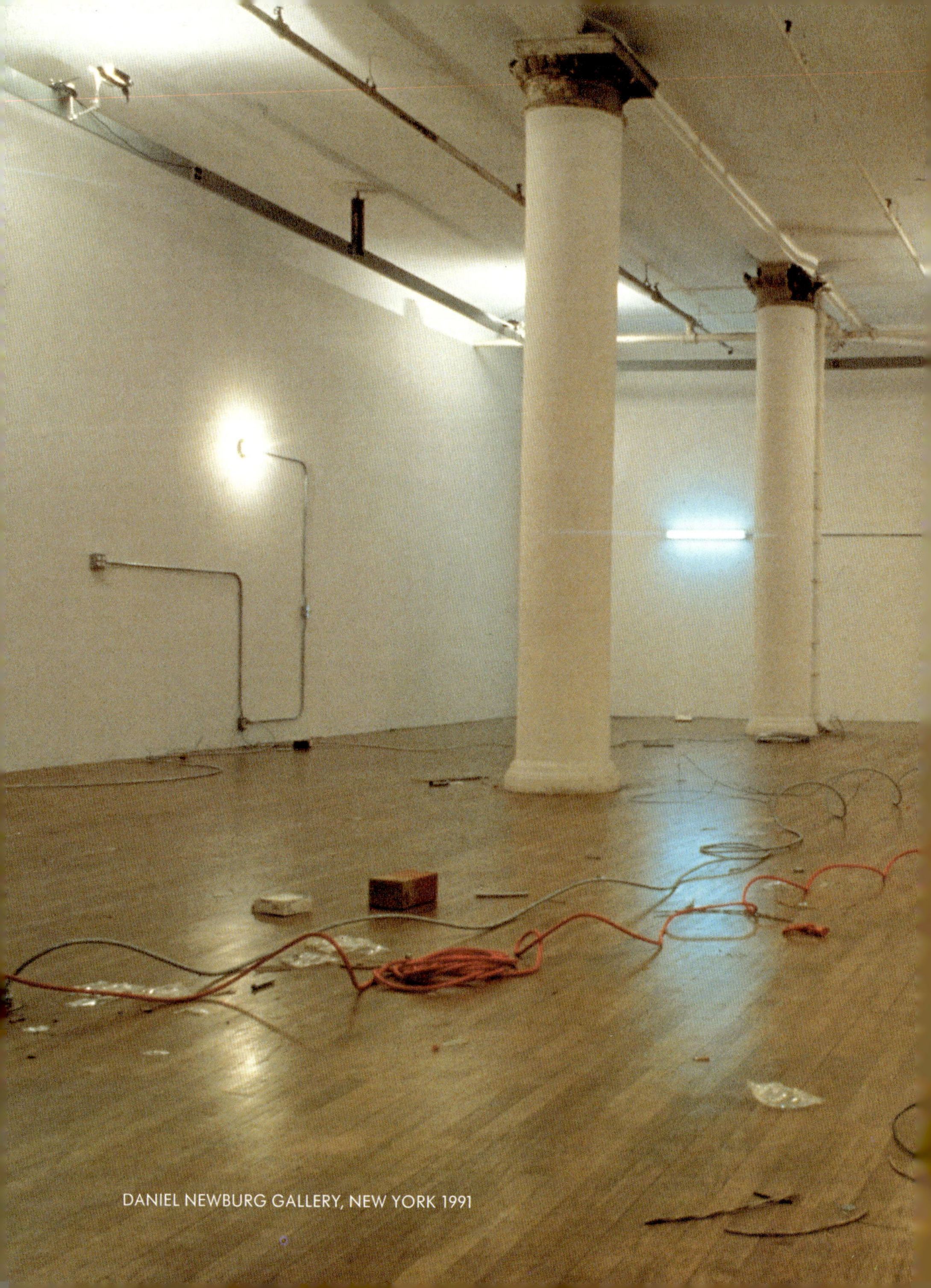
DANIEL NEWBURG GALLERY, NEW YORK 1991

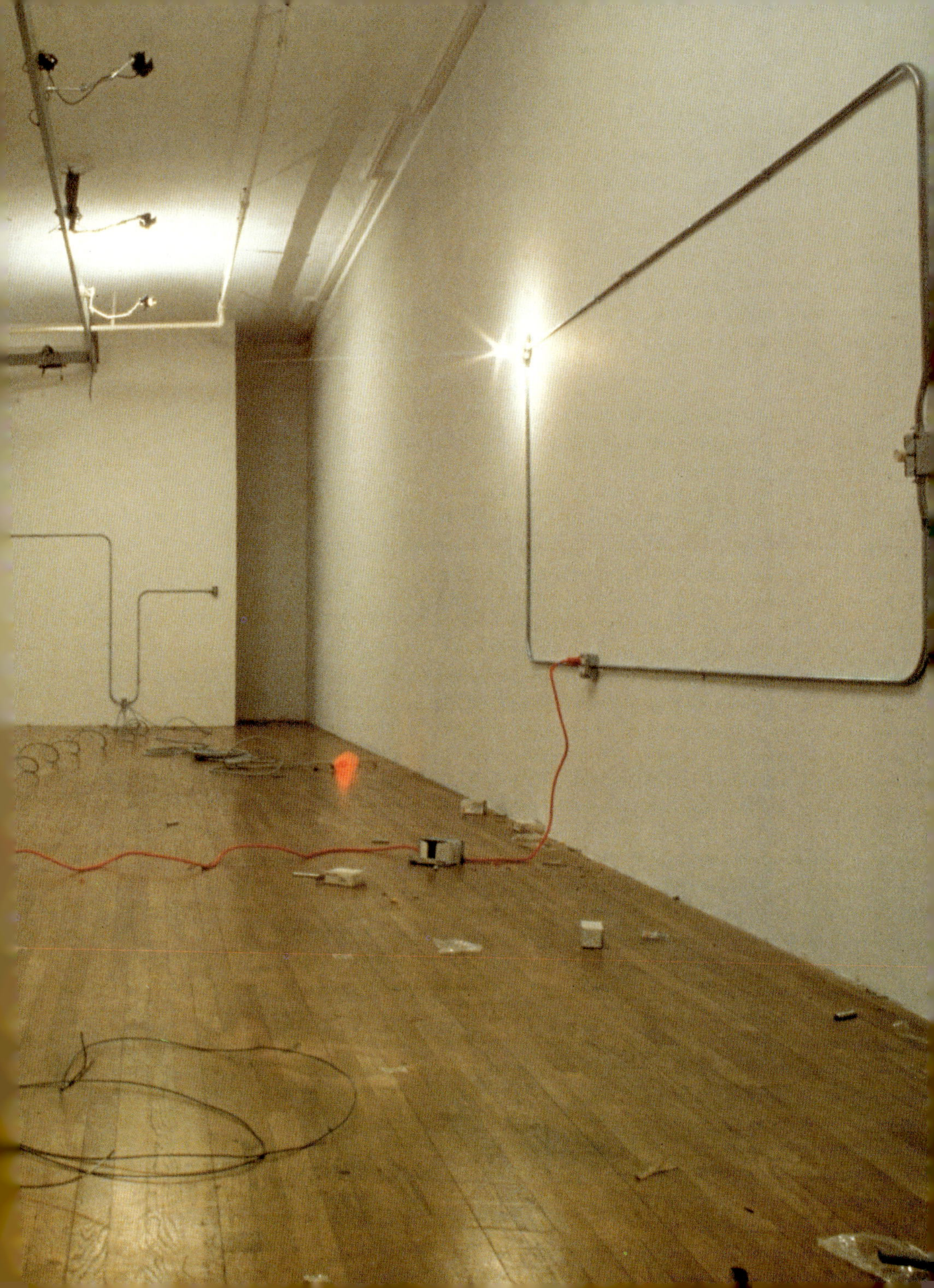

schen Thema werden. In den scheinbar spontan und zufällig über den gesamten Raum ausgelegten Kabelsträngen werden diese Energieströme als ein zwischen allen Zentren der Installation gespanntes und verzweigtes Versorgungssystem visuell erfahrbar. Gleichzeitig strahlen die Glühlampen Energien in Form von Licht und Wärme ab, während die Ventilatoren eine spürbare Windenergie erzeugen. Die ebenfalls an diesen Stromkreis angeschlossenen Kassetten- und Videogeräte wiederum geben als Ton- und Bildsequenzen gespeicherte, durch menschliche Kraftanstrengungen erzeugte Energien ab. Aus Lautsprechertürmen schlägt dem Ausstellungsbesucher der frenetische, tausendfache Jubel einer riesigen Menschenmenge entgegen. Und auf den Monitoren in McCaslins aktueller, für das Sprengel Museum Hannover eingerichteter Installation sieht sich der Betrachter mit einer ziellos durch ein Labyrinth unendlicher Gänge stürzenden Gestalt konfrontiert. Gegen den statischen Charakter des Materials setzt McCaslin also den kontinuierlichen Fluß elektrischer Energien, die unter anderem eine enervierende Geräuschkulisse und eine sich ständig repetierende Flut nahezu identischer Bildsequenzen erzeugen. Von den in die Objekte und Installationen integrierten elektrischen »Standarduhren« werden diese Energieströme in Form abgelaufener Zeit präzise gemessen.

Matthew McCaslins Ausstellungen sind auf eine experimentelle Situation reduzierte ästhetische Modelle komplexer energetischer Zustände. Seine in einem Netzwerk verbundenen Arrangements industrieller Materialien werden dabei zu Bildmetaphern globaler technischer, ökologischer und humaner Energien und ihres maßlosen Verbrauchs.

Dietmar Elger

NETWORKS OF ART
The Exhibitions of Matthew McCaslin

A certain transience is immanent in the installations of Matthew McCaslin. The exhibitions initially tend to aggravate visitors by shattering the museum-goer's expectations: those who enter the presentation area are confronted with what is ostensibly a construction site. The installations simulate a condition of permanent upheaval. Electric cables snake back and forth aross the floor; a ceiling element has been lowered, revealing the hidden architectural structure, and appears to be the first step in some repair work (Figure pp. 14|15). In like fashion, the aluminium grid brace cutting through the room is apparently the forerunner of a dividing wall yet to be completed (Fig. p. 6). Cast about the floor are bits and pieces of cable, plastic caps and extra screws, the traces of hard work in progress.

In his installations, Matthew McCaslin uncovers the otherwise invisible infrastructure of the exhibition site's architecture to reinstate it in that same space as an artistic instrument with a new, aesthetic function. The interior construction of the site — i.e. the industrial metal gridwork and intermediate ceillings with their comprehensive electric supply system of cables, light switches, plugs and open mountings — is the basic material to which McCaslin adds requisite ventilators, meters and audio-visual equipment.

The installations Matthew McCaslin devises for his exhibitions convert the entire room, complete with its specific architectonic qualities, into a temporary aesthetic situation remaining in existence for the space of only a few weeks. The artist's projects for the Jennifer Flay Gallery in Paris in 1991 (Fig. pp. 14|15) and the New York Museum of Modern Art the year after (Fig. p. 25) are prime examples. Yet McCaslin is also interested in developing autonomous sculptural pieces — via his work for exhibitions and initially integrated in them — which are not exclusively contingent on a specific installation. Distributed throughout the room, these constitute the artistic centers of each presentation, and it is these focal centers which McCaslin combines and connects with a densely woven and manifestly unorganized tangle of cables to comprise an interactive network. A single switch usually controls the energy flow to all the works, and interrupting that one current suffices to shut down the entire light and media complex. The centers located within the installations, those focal points at which McCaslin

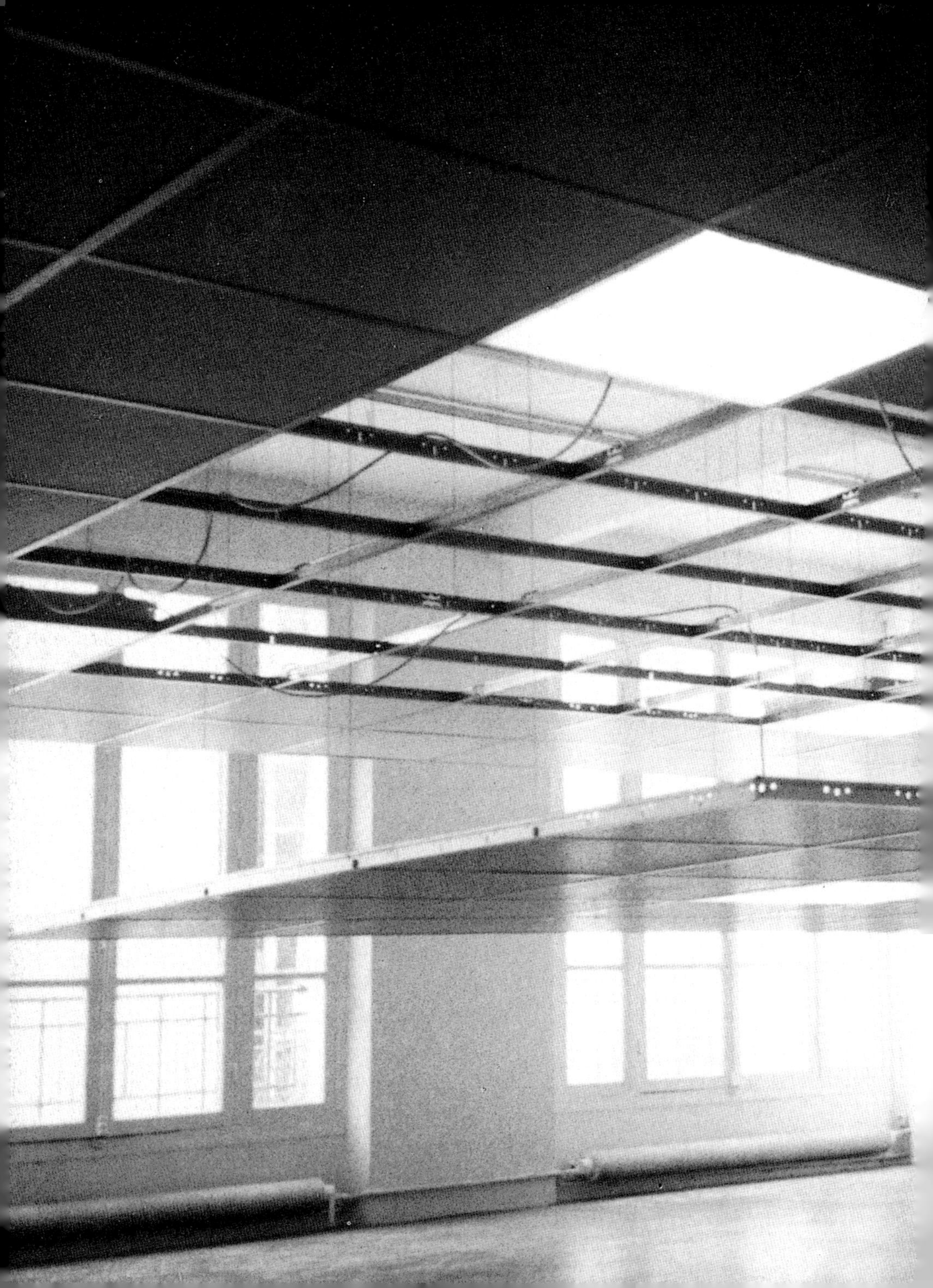

THE SKY IS FALLING, GALERIE JENNIFER FLAY, PARIS 1991

consolidates his industrial materials to form complicated arrangements, gain in this process an aesthetic charge ensuring their existence as self-sufficient and mobile sculptural works beyond the limited lifespan of the exhibition itself. Only seldom, in contrast, are works actually executed at the artist's New York studio. That site mainly serves the purpose of a laboratory during the preparation stage, a place where McCaslin is able to simulate and test certain ideas or details of an exhibition concept. Conversely, the exhibition rooms of galleries and museums function as a type of temporary studio to be occupied by the artist only for a certain length of time. It is there, following an intensive preparatory phase and under the time pressure of an imminent opening, that his objects evolve "on-site," formed out of infinite meters of extensions cords and countless connecting plugs that fuse finally into a dense power supply system.

As a result of this approach, the exhibitions give rise to work groups which exhibit common characteristics by virtue of their identical materials and related formal vocabulary. A seemingly chaotic clutter of twisted and bundled cables with multiple plugs, switches and reflecting filament bulbs is characteristic, for instance, of the objects from the 1992 presentation in the Cologne Rolf Ricke Gallery (Fig. pp. 22|23); while simple geometric forms and work arrangements with integrated audio-visual equipment and striking sound and picture impulses are indicative of the installations in 1991 (Fig. pp. 10|11) and 1993 (Fig. pp. 30|31) at Daniel Newburg's gallery in New York.

Rarely does McCaslin give his exhibitions titles. Only the concentrated object arrangements slated to live on as independent works are given ironic, richly associative names such as "48 Hours In A Day," "Path of Least Resistance," "Revolution," or "Love Letter." These titles are often a direct outgrown of the process of creation/production itself; whereas other, more literary designations frequently evolve from very private experiences.

It is not without a certain mischievous gesture that McCaslin arranges his materials to form anarchic compositions that ironically undermine the strict functionality and practical efficiency of the standard meters, light switches, splices and ventilators composing them. This aesthetic approach bears the stamp of Matthew McCaslin's experiences and contact with the now historic artistic postures of the 'sixties. Today, two decades later, he has revived these postures by re-declining their formal language, recasting them with current topics and hence rendering them new postures in their own right. Here McCaslin's concept

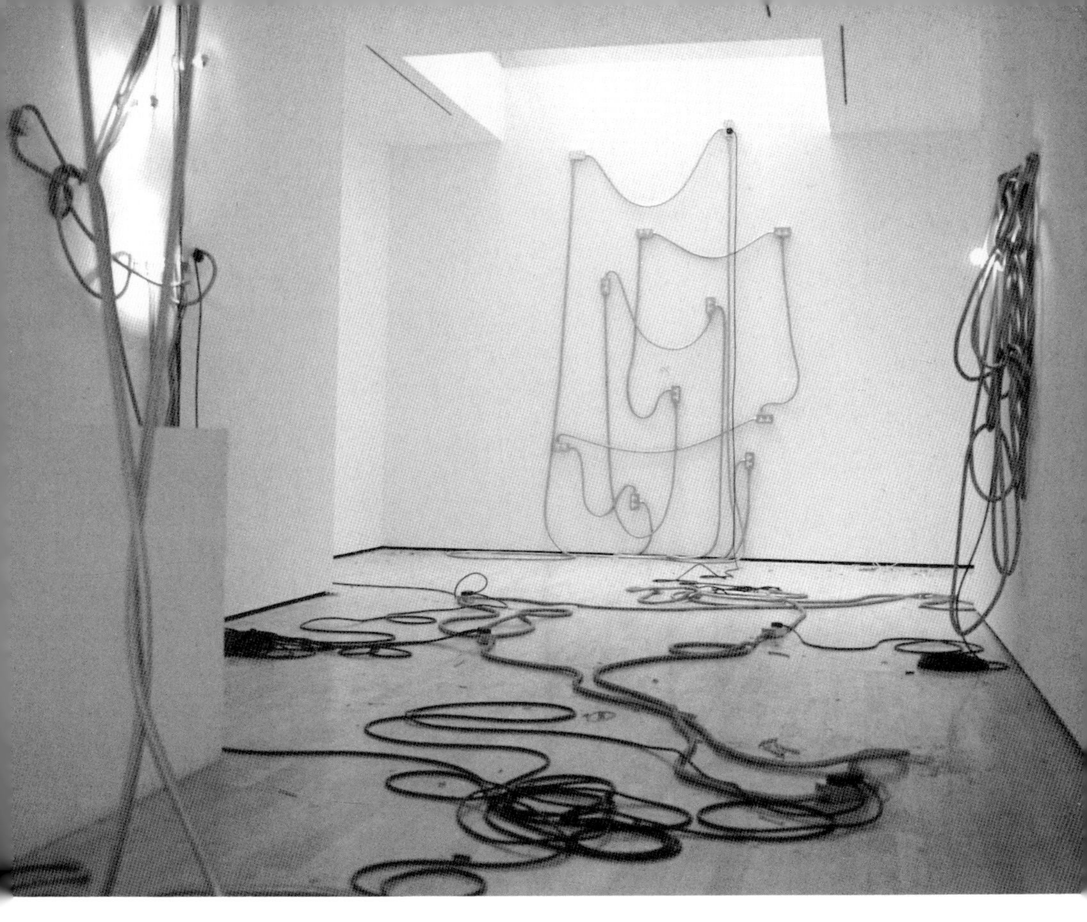

ANTHONY REYNOLDS GALLERY, LONDON 1991

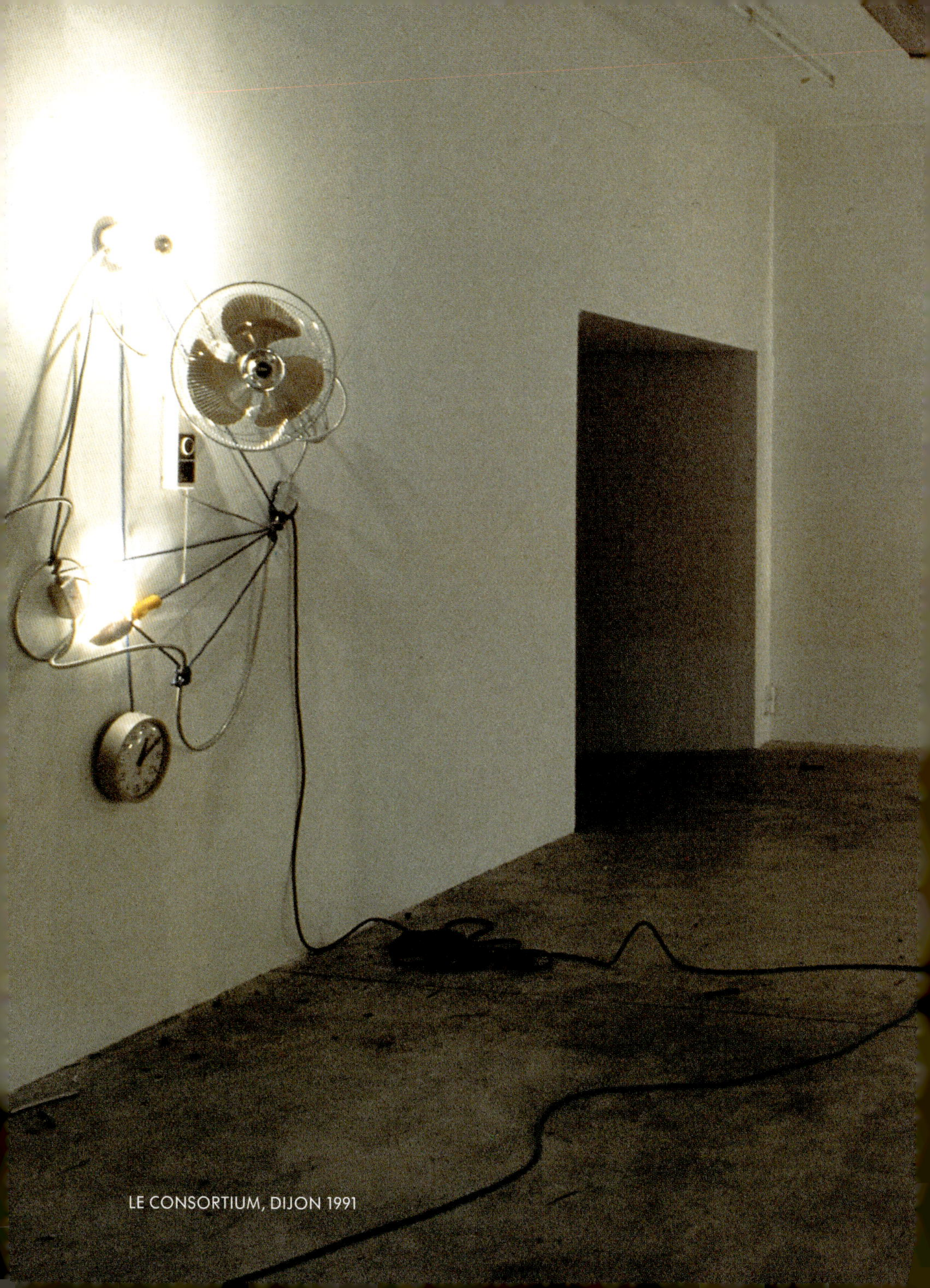

LE CONSORTIUM, DIJON 1991

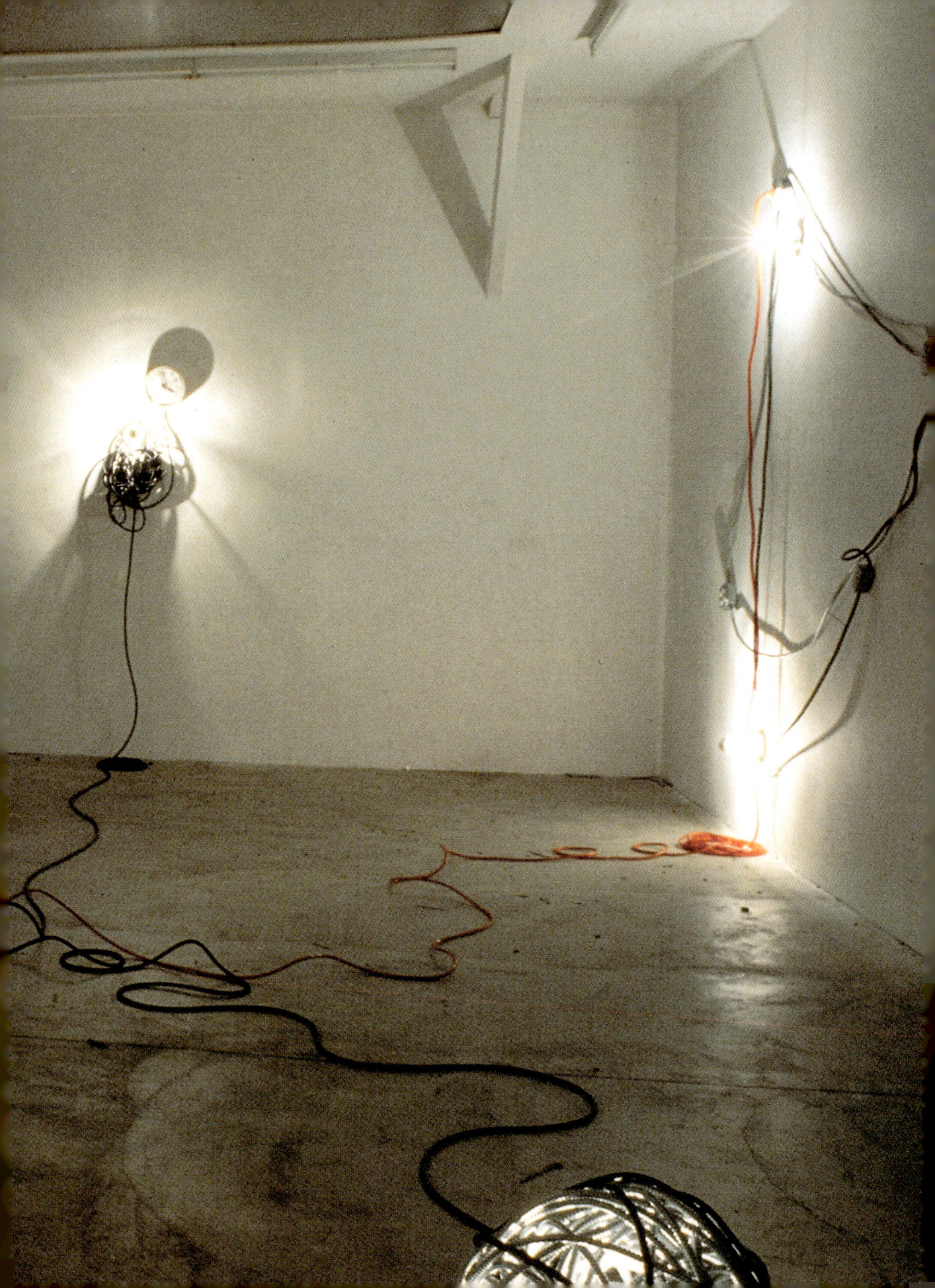

overlaps with that of other artists of his generation such as Matthew Barney, Felix Gonzalez-Torres, Thom Merrick, Cady Noland and Jessica Stockholder.

Matthew McCaslin's works also bear witness to several characteristic gestalt principles of postminimalist sculpture in that they visibly refrain from precisely structured composition. Instead, they allow the material sufficient leeway to let coincidence and chaos determine each installation's provisional character. The cable splices, switches and multiple plugs do more than merely supply the power necessary to make the lamps, meters and ventilators function. They lay claim to equality and a separate existence as aesthetic material within the process of creation.

The tradition of early objects and installations by Bruce Nauman and Keith Sonnier sheds an explanatory light on McCaslin's aim of presenting a challenge while going further to confront his audience with a wealth of different stimulants keyed to activate several sensory organs simultaneously. The purely visual presence of the objects undergoes an intensification by means of bright, glittering lights and media images alternating in a fast-paced rhythm. McCaslin provides loud signals as an acoustic complement, and even enables visitors to sensually perceive his art in the form of wind power generated by the ventilators. A visitor strolling through the installation will become an integral part of the exhibition. His presence and his movements in the room can alter the work: when he passes photoelectric barries, he triggers acoustic signals; by shifting a single switch, he can interrupt the installation's entire electric power circuit.

The industrially-produced materials with their reduced functionalism and technical surfaces do link Matthew McCaslin's work to the aesthetics of various minimalistic approaches. Yet the energies flowing through these largely static objects constitute the real material of McCaslin's art, and their flow, exchange and loss constitute the artistic theme. The cable lengths criss-crossing the entire room in seemingly spontaneous and arbitrary disorder render the energy currents visual: a supply system connecting and interconnecting all the centers of the installation. At the same time, the bulbs emanate energy in the form of light and heat; the ventilators produce palpable gusts of wind power. The cassette and video equipment hooked onto this circuit contributes audio-visual sequences, the products of manmade energy. Loudspeakers bombard visitors with the frenetic cheering of a huge, frenzied crowd. And the monitors in this installation for the Hanover Sprengel Museum confront the viewer with a disoriented figure lurching through a labyrinth of infinite pathways. McCaslin contrasts the static character of the material with the continuous flow of electric power generating, among other things, an unrelenting backdrop of noise and a flood of nearly identical picture sequences shown in constant repetition. The standard meters integrated in the objects and installations clock and measure these energy currents in precise increments of passing time.

Matthew McCaslin's exhibitions are aesthetic models of complex energy constellations reduced to an experimental situation. His arrangements of industrial materials, constituting as they do a network, are rendered pictorial metaphors for global technological, ecological and human energies and their uninhibited consumption.

Dietmar Elger

Translated from the German by Mary Fran Gilbert

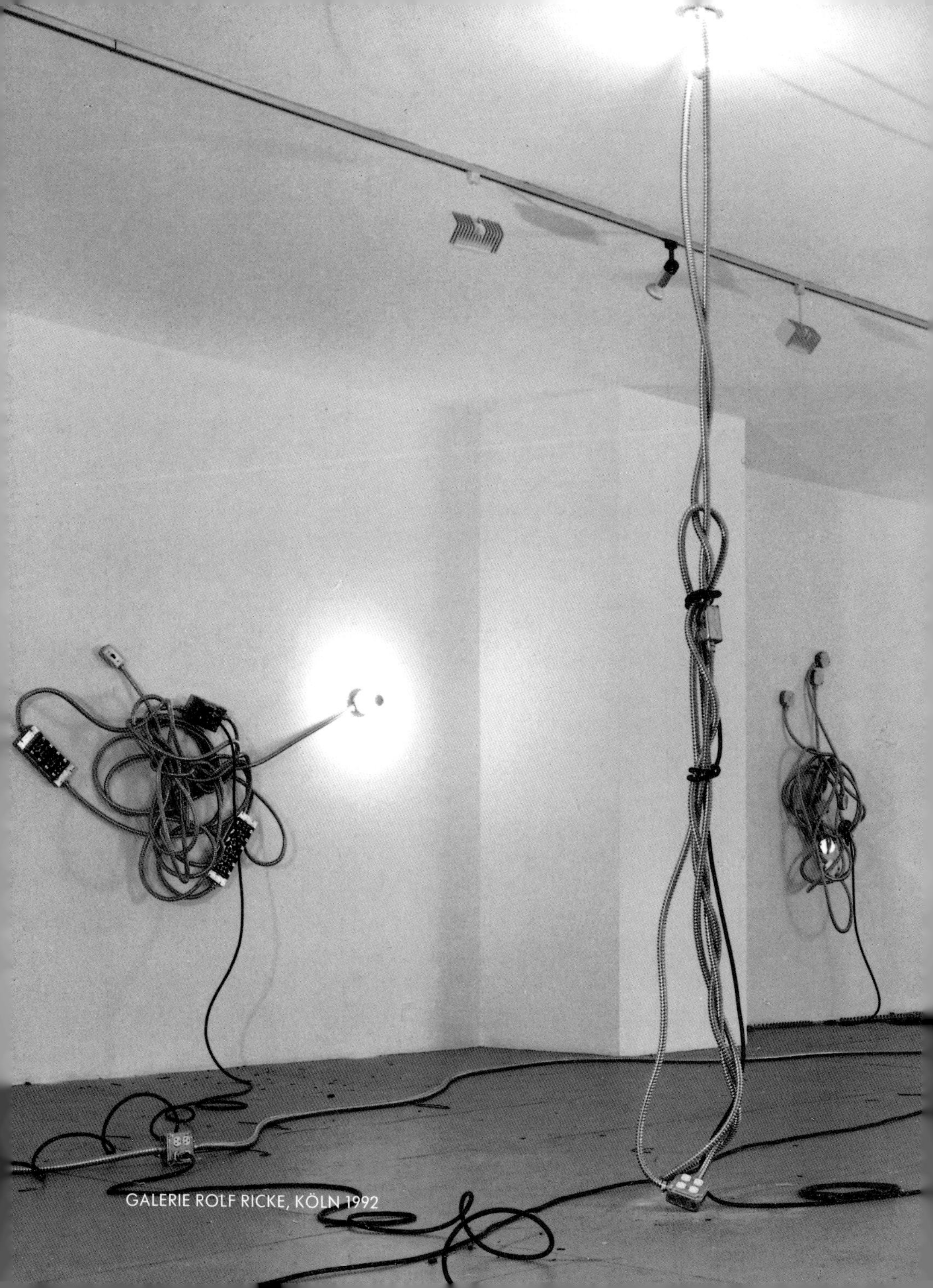

GALERIE ROLF RICKE, KÖLN 1992

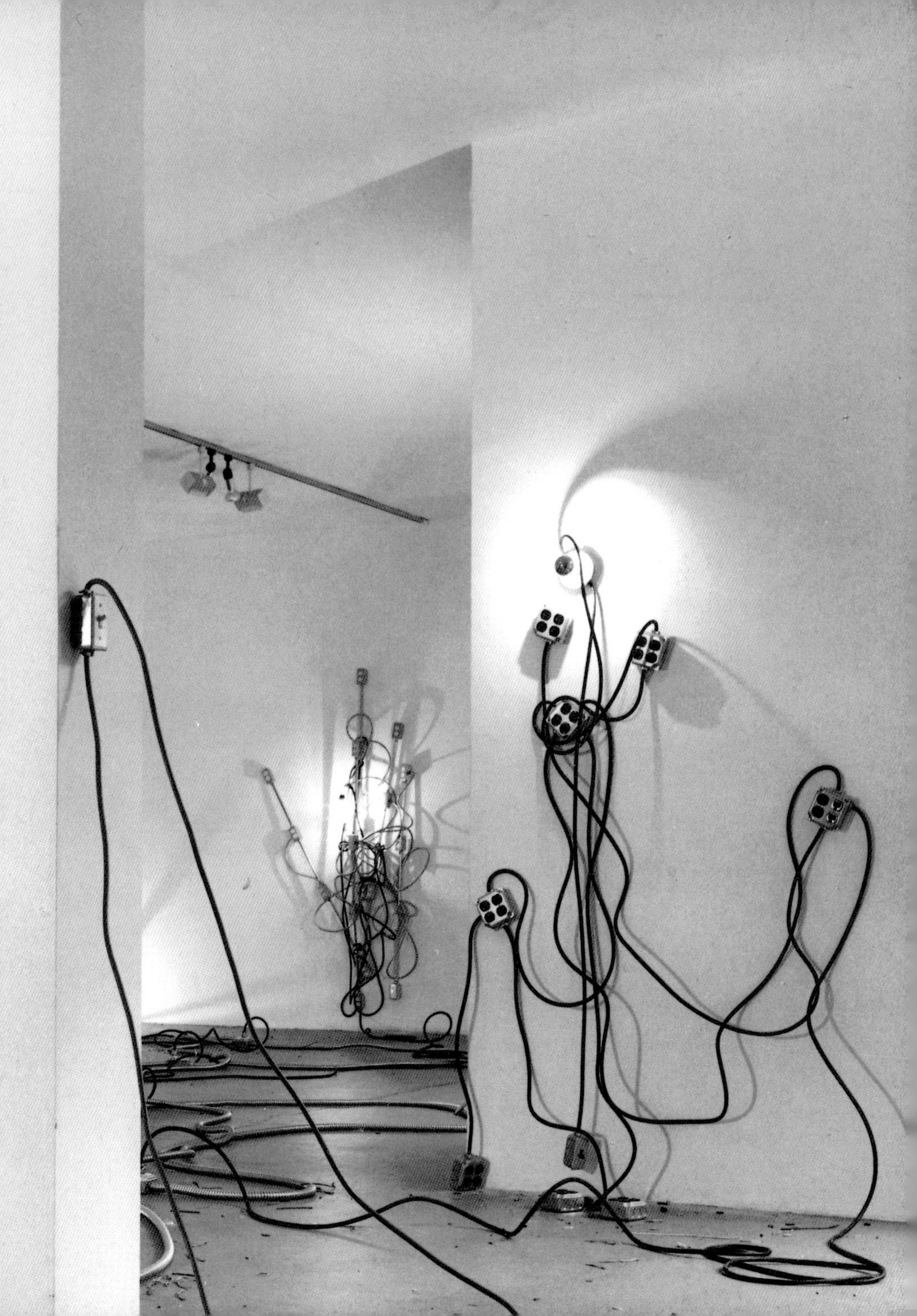

»PANTA RHEI«
Zu den Arbeiten von Matthew McCaslin

Ein Gewirr aus Kabeln, ein paar Uhren an der Wand; Radios, wie zufällig auf dem Boden abgestellt und vergessen; Stecker, aus denen Kabelstücke heraushängen… Auf den ersten Blick erscheinen die Arbeiten von Matthew McCaslin wie unfertige oder noch im Entstehen begriffene, wenig *kunstvolle* Arrangements alltäglicher Banalitäten.

Doch gehört dieses schon klassische Mißverständnis der Wahrnehmung moderner Kunst — von Marcel Duchamps Pissoirbecken und Meret Oppenheims bepelzter Teetasse über Daniel Spoerris eingefrorene Tischmenüreste und Claes Oldenburgs Mausmuseum bis zu der Badewanne von Joseph Beuys, den Brillo-Boxen von Andy Warhol oder den Resträumen von Peter Fischli und David Weiss — zu den »common sense«-Erfahrungen ausstellungsgestählter Kunstliebhaber. Der kulturelle Code, der in der Verfremdung und Translokation banaler Gegenstände in den auratischen Zusammenhang von Galerie und Museumsräumen den eigentlichen, sich selbst bereits genügenden kreativen Akt zu erkennen vermag, funktioniert zunächst auch bei Matthew McCaslin. Kalkuliert surreale Betitelungen verrätseln und verdeutlichen zugleich den künstlerischen Traditionszusammenhang seiner Arbeiten.

Matthew McCaslin benutzt technisches Equipment wie andere Künstler Pinsel und Farbe. Er komponiert und arrangiert mit diesen Materialien Ereignisse, Environments im Raum. Diese beziehen sich jeweils sehr bewußt auf die vorgefundenen Raumsituationen. Aus Kabeln und Drähten, aus Metallgestängen und Uhren entstehen so temporäre Anordnungen, die den Räumen das zurückgeben, was wir üblicherweise von und in ihnen eben nicht sehen: ihr energetisches Gerüst, ihr Innenleben, versteckt hinter Wänden.

Jahrelang war McCaslin als Bauarbeiter beschäftigt, um seine Kunst zu finanzieren. Der künstlerische Aussagemodus der »Installationen« ist insofern bei ihm wortwörtlich zu nehmen: Er bedient sich aus diesen Erfahrungen heraus der *Eingeweide*, der technologischen Skelette jener Energiesysteme, die heute für jedes Gebäude konstitutiv sind. In der Architektur selbst spricht man von »smart buildings« oder »intelligent buildings« immer dann, wenn die in Böden, Decken und Wänden eingezogenen technischen Systeme für Informations- und Wärmeübertragung einem avancierten High-Tech-Level entsprechen. McCaslin benutzt

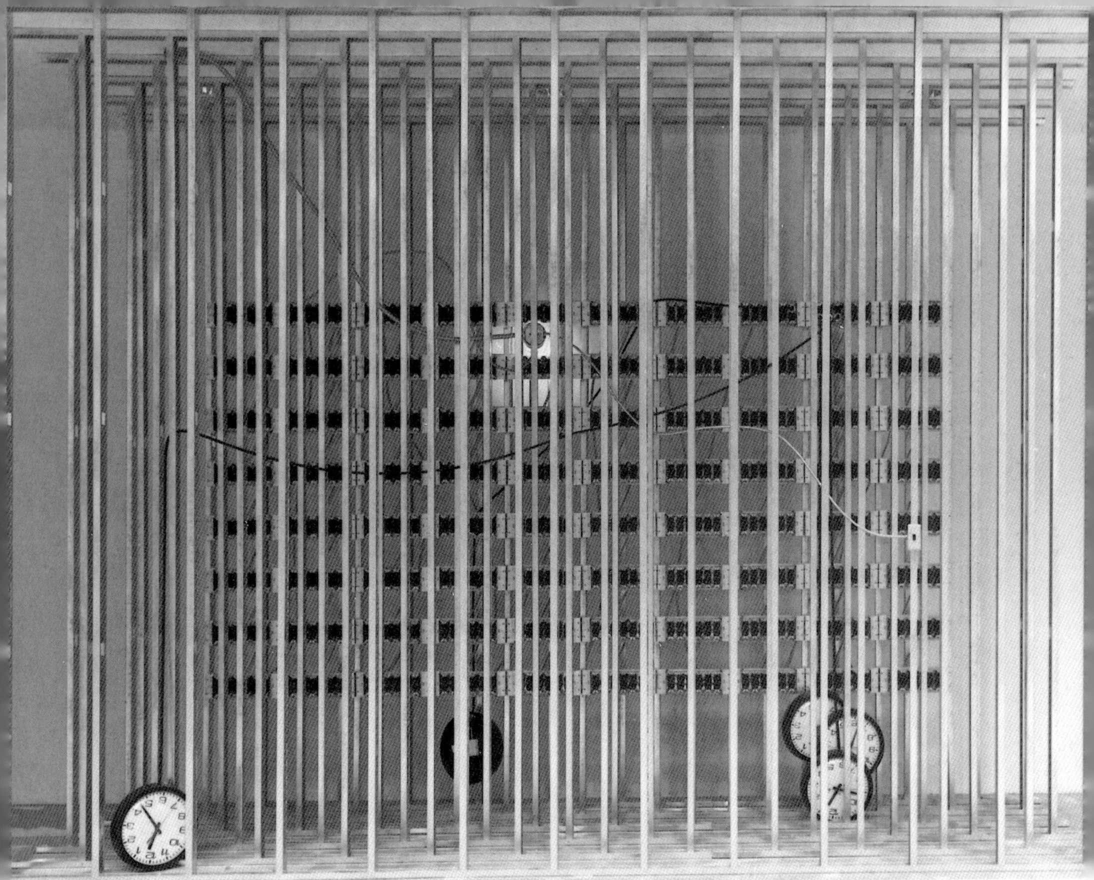

TRIBUTE TO A MOMENT, THE MUSEUM OF MODERN ART, NEW YORK 1992

diese Systeme, aber er transzendiert sie zugleich, indem er sie transloziert und offen zeigt.

Die Kabel, Drähte und Uhren, frei an der Wand oder auf dem Boden arrangiert, bekommen dabei gleich in mehrfacher Hinsicht magische Dingqualität. Sie weisen über sich selbst hinaus.

Die verschlungenen Kabel geben sich als *Eingeweide*, als Innenleben der Gebäude zu erkennen. Eine animistische Sicht, die durchaus auch ihre logische, nicht nur metaphorische Evidenz hat, wenn man bedenkt, daß auch Informationen, für die Kabel der materielle Träger sind, *verdaut* werden müssen. Sie können *verträglich* oder *unverträglich* sein. Aber die Verkabelung, die Verdrahtung, ist auch Metapher für eine Informationsgesellschaft, die in Chips und Megabytes denkt und für die der Computer, das *Netz* zur Bedingung und zum Garanten ihres Funktionierens geworden ist. Nicht nur die Konsumption, sondern zunehmend auch die Produktion wird durch Informationsübermittlung bestimmt. Sowohl die künstliche als auch die natürliche biologische Informationsvermittlung wird bereits in eins gedacht: Bioenergetics, Biophysik, Biochemie, Gentechnik, »Virtual Reality« sind hier die Bezugsgrößen. Neueste Konstruktionsstrategien arbeiten biomimetisch: Flugzeugtragflächen orientieren sich an der mikrobiologischen Konstruktion von Insektenflügeln, Funk-Spionage und Echolot von Schiffen imitieren die Wahrnehmungssysteme von Fledermäusen.

Daß das *Künstliche* und das *Natürliche* keine distinkten Realitätsebenen bleiben müssen, wurde spätestens seit der »Biotronik« bekannt, der zuerst in der literarischen Gattung der Science-Fiction ausformulierten Vorstellung, daß die Schnittstellen zwischen Mensch und Maschine fließende Übergänge werden können. Weit über die narrative Präsenz hinaus haben solche Szenarios, zu Ende gedacht, einschneidende Konsequenzen für die Philosophie, speziell die Erkenntnistheorie. Daß Technik und Technologie magische Qualitäten haben, wird auch dadurch deutlich, daß wir sie in aller Regel unreflektiert, lediglich instrumentell benutzen, gedankenlos, fast unbewußt. Ein Zahnrad, eine Pleuelstange, ein Keilriemen zeigen in ihrer Gestalt, wie sie funktionieren, welche Kräfte wirksam werden. Dagegen sind Stromkabel, Chips oder digitale Uhrwerke in ihren technischen Bedingungen und Abläufen unanschaulich. Es bewegt sich optisch und faktisch nichts, aber trotzdem wird Energie übertragen. Das bleibt einer mechanistischen Logik schwer verständlich.

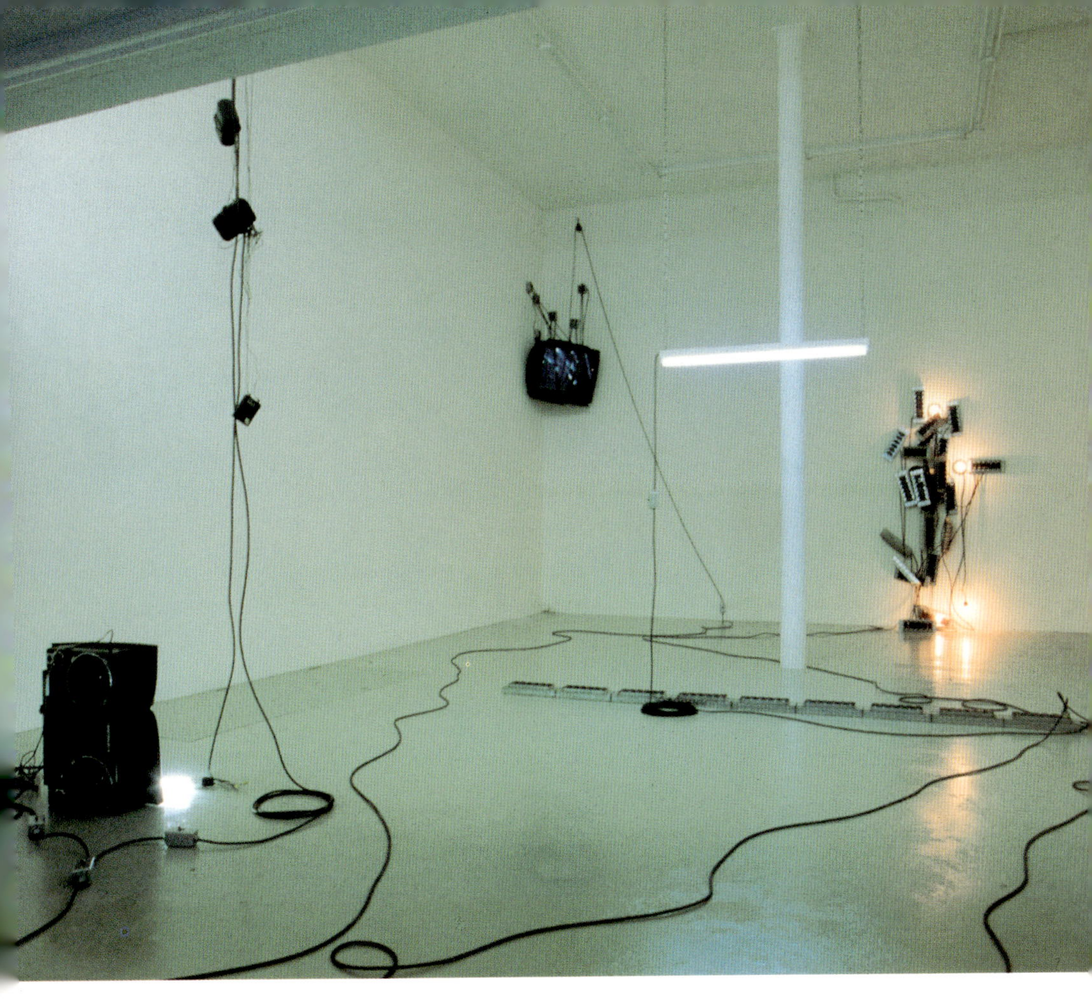

ART & PUBLIC, GENF 1992

Mit all diesen Beziehungsgefügen setzen sich McCaslins Installationen auseinander. Seine ästhetische Erkenntnisarbeit besteht darin, daß er die Reste, die Artefakte, die »objets trouvés« energetischer Kraft- und Informationsübertragung im Koordinatensystem einer mechanistischen Logik präsentiert. Damit verhalten sich Form und Funktion gegenläufig oder sind zumindest gegeneinander verschoben. Der Aussagemodus seiner Installationen hinterfragt das fraglose Funktionieren, indem er die Funktionen ad absurdum führt, frei nach Francis Picabia: »Der Kopf ist rund, damit das Denken seine Richtung ändern kann.« Die technischen (Bau-)Reste der Kabel und Drähte, Gitter und Schalter werden bei McCaslin in der vollen Wortbedeutung sur-real, weil sie eine magische Funktion jenseits ihrer üblichen Verwendung beschwören. Und ähnlich wie die Surrealisten gibt Matthew McCaslin seinen Installationen metaphorisch-magische Titel wie »Fischeye Jungle«, »See Spot Run« oder »My Shoes Are Smiling«. Die zuletzt genannte Arbeit besteht aus sechs auf den Boden gestellten Ghetto-Blastern, die untereinander verkabelt sind, und durch eine überdimensionale Glühbirne, die zwischen diesen Radiogeräten liegt, magisches Schlagschattenlicht erhält. Gleichermaßen ist hier die Vorstellung der Welt als »globales Dorf«, das nur noch aus zeitgleichen ortsunabhängigen Informationen besteht, und eine Ghetto-Jugendkultur angesprochen, die sich die Ohren zudröhnt, weil sie keine gesellschaftliche Perspektive mehr hat. Das, was in den Kabeln fließt, die Energie, die Töne, die Informationen, ist materiell und immateriell zugleich. Energetische Ströme sind meßbar, regelbar. Und diese Ströme sind zunehmend das Regelsystem für Welt und Gesellschaft. Insofern ist McCaslins Thematisierung energetischer Ströme gewissermaßen die amerikanische, pragmatische Antwort auf die Energievorstellungen eines Joseph Beuys, wie sie sich etwa in der »Honigpumpe« konkretisierten.

Die Meßbarkeit des Immateriellen oder zumindest unseren Wunsch danach betonen aber auch die Uhren, jene Chronographen, die der Künstler so oft und auffallend in seine Installationen integriert. Häufig miteinander verkabelt und mit Reglern, Steckdosen oder »technical units« komplettiert, focussieren sie die gegenwärtige Manie der Zeitmessung. Tausendstel Sekunden entscheiden über sportlichen Erfolg, »acht Stunden sind kein Tag«, Stechuhren, Zeitzünder an Bomben. Noch der Weltuntergang wird am liebsten mit der Metapher der Uhr ausgedrückt, auf der es, je nach Einschätzung, »fünf vor zwölf« oder bereits »fünf nach zwölf« ist. Daß Zeit verrinnt, unwiderbringlich ist, daß sie gewissermaßen *tropft*, hatten schon die Surrealisten thematisiert. Andererseits hat erst seit und mit der exakten Zeitmessung das »Zeitalter der Moderne« – in sozialer, technologischer, kultureller und logischer Hinsicht – begonnen. Begriffe wie »Messen« und »Vermessen« sind nicht nur etymologisch eng miteinander verwandt. Die Rationalität des Zollstocks, der Uhr, des rechten Winkels – Faktoren, die unter andere eben auch für heutige Bautechnik konstitutiv sind – ist hyperrational geworden, entbehrt oft nicht der Hybris. Und so lassen sich auch McCaslins Drähte und Uhren, Lautsprecher und Glühbirnen als Indikatoren für eine Erweiterung unserer Sinne (unserer Sinnlichkeit?) interpretieren, die zum Guten wie zum Schlechten sich wenden kann. Strom ermöglicht Wärme, aber auch Folter; Licht erweitert den Tag, aber es gibt auch Lichtverschmutzung; Ton- und Bildübertragung erlauben uns, am Geschehen der Welt, vom klassischen Konzert bis zum Boxkampf, von der Himalaya-Expedition bis zur Mondlandung, teilzunehmen. Aber Bild und Ton entmündigen uns auch, wenn sie inflationär und ubiquitär auftreten. Bericht und Kommentar, eigene und gespiegelte Meinung werden unterscheidbar, und zunehmend werden die Fakten fiktional angereichert: »Reality TV«, »Infotainment«, Nachrichtensendungen, so das Ergebnis neuerer Rezeptionsuntersuchungen, bekommen zunehmend die Qualität von »Hintergrundrauschen«. Alles, aber auch wirklich alles, kann »Public Relation« werden und wird es auch.

Auch auf dieser Ebene setzen Matthew McCaslins Installationen an, auch und gerade weil sie nicht mit High-Tech-Equipment auftrumpfen wie viele der künstlerischen Installationen der sogenannten »Neuen Medien«. Im Gegenteil: sie sind karg bis hin zu einer calvinistischen Nüchternheit. Erst dadurch aber zwingen sie unsere Wahrnehmung, die »essentials« hochkomplexer, künstlicher Weltverfassung zu beachten, zu beobachten. McCaslins Arbeiten haben, gerade weil sie keine, zumindest keine eindeutigen Geschichten erzählen, die Evidenz eines »Haiku«, jener japanische Gedichtform, die es vermag, in nur drei Zeilen einen komplexen Gedankengang zusammenzufassen. Es sind ontologische Gerüste von Zeit- und Technikwahrnehmung, abstrakt und konkret zugleich.

Im Gewand äußerster Absichtslosigkeit zeigt sich eine kalkulierte Absicht; das Chaos hat und erzeugt eine inhärente Ordnung. »Die Welt am Draht«, um einen Filmtitel von Fassbinder zu zitieren, bekommt in McCaslins Installationen eine konkrete, aber auch magische Qualität. Ihre Bedeutungsvielfalt, ihr komplexes Verweissystem an Assoziationen läßt sich mit einem Satz von Guillaume Apolli-

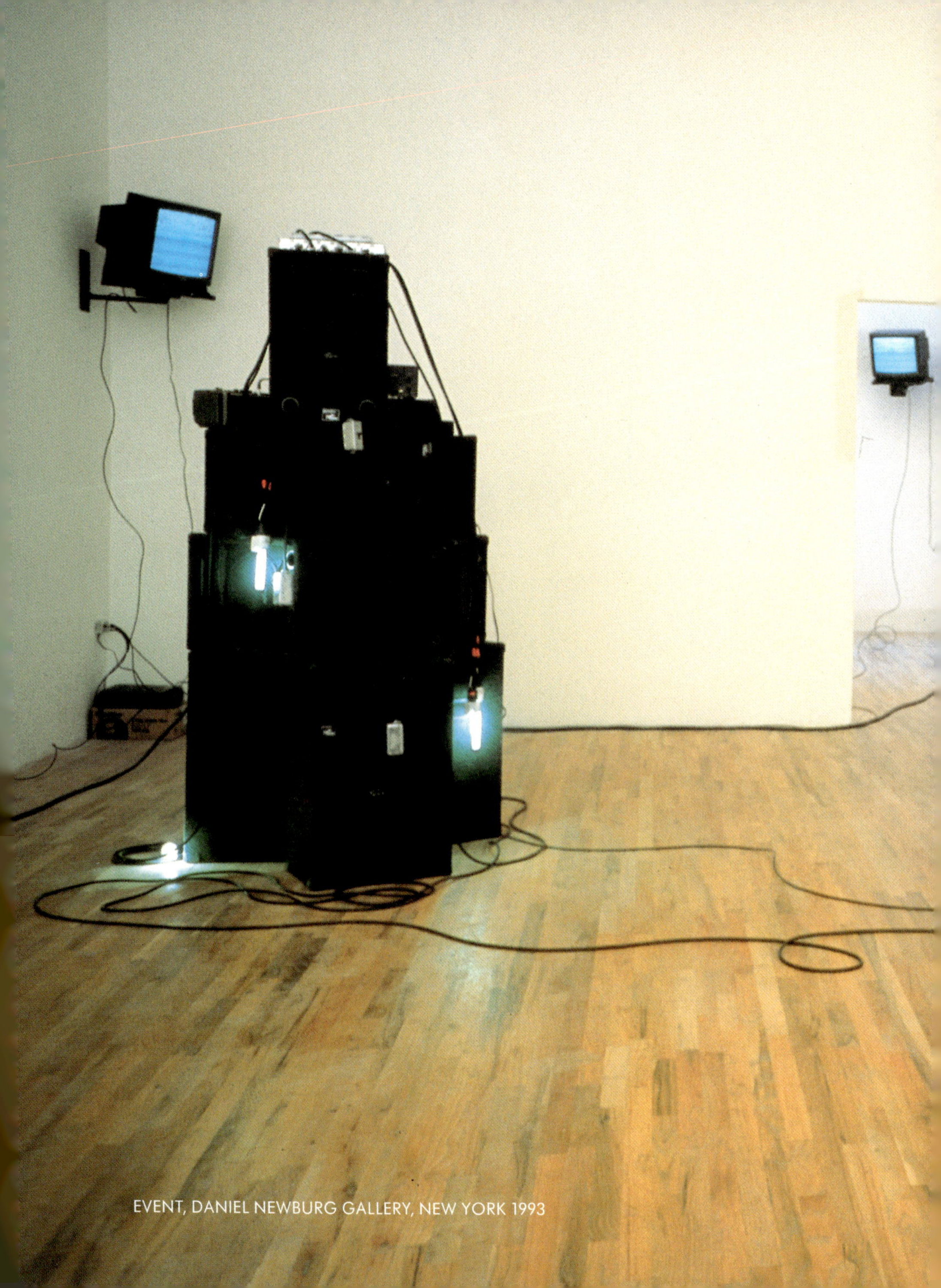

EVENT, DANIEL NEWBURG GALLERY, NEW YORK 1993

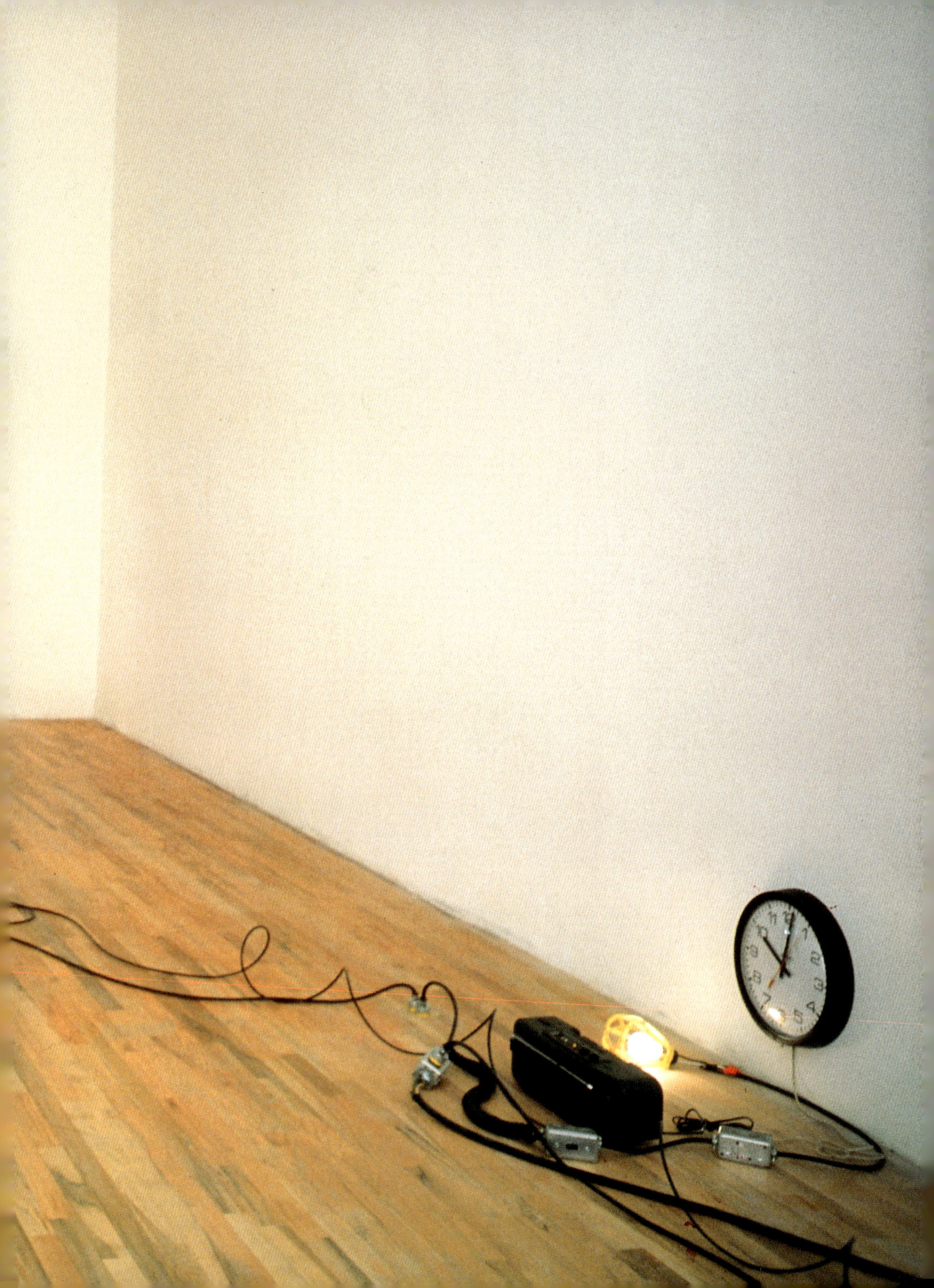

naire zusammenfassen: »Der Weise lacht nur mit Zittern.« Und bezogen auf die energetischen Ströme, die auch die Entropie als die grundlegende Konstante von Welt und Sein überhaupt benennen, wußte schon Heraklit daraus ein Realitätsgesetz abzuleiten: »panta rhei« – »alles fließt«.

Anna Meseure

»PANTA RHEI«
On Matthew McCaslin's Work

A tangle of cables, a few meters on the wall; radios standing on the floor as if put down for a moment and forgotten; plugs from which loose cable ends protrude… At first glance, these works by Matthew McCaslin appear to be unfinished or still in-progress, and none too *artful* arrangements of everyday banality.

Yet this by now classic misconception in the perception modern art – be it Marcel Duchamp's pissoir, Meret Oppenheim's furry teacup, Daniel Spoerri's frozen leftovers, Claes Oldenburg's mouse museum, Joseph Beuy's bathtub, Andy Warhol's Brillo boxes or the spare spaces by Peter Fischli and David Weiss – it belongs to the "common-sense" experiences of exhibition-steeled art-lovers. Initially, Matthew McCaslin's works can also be interpreted according to that cultural code which perceives the alienation and translocation of banal items placed in the aura-like museum context as the self-contained and self-satisfying creative act per se. Calculatedly surrealistic titles both enigmatize and elucidate the artistic traditions underlying his work.

Matthew McCaslin implements technical equipment as other artists implement brushes and paint. Using these materials, he composes and arranges events and environments within space. These refer very deliberately to given spatial constellations. Cables, wires, metal rods and meters are combined to form temporary systems which restore to the rooms what we usually fail to see of and in them: their energetic parameters, their inner life, concealed behind walls.

For many years McCaslin did construction work to finance his art. The artistic mode of expression called "installation" is thus quite literally applicable. Drawing from his experience, he uses the *bowels,* the technological skeleton inside the energy systems forming an integral component of every modern building. The language of architecture itself refers to "smart" or "intelligent buildings" whenever the technical information and ventilation systems installed within the floors, walls and ceilings meet the advanced requirements of high-tech. McCaslin simultaneously implements and transcends these systems by showing them translocated and naked.

The cables, wires and meters, arranged freely on the wall or floor, gain a magic object quality in a number of ways. They signify something beyond themselves.

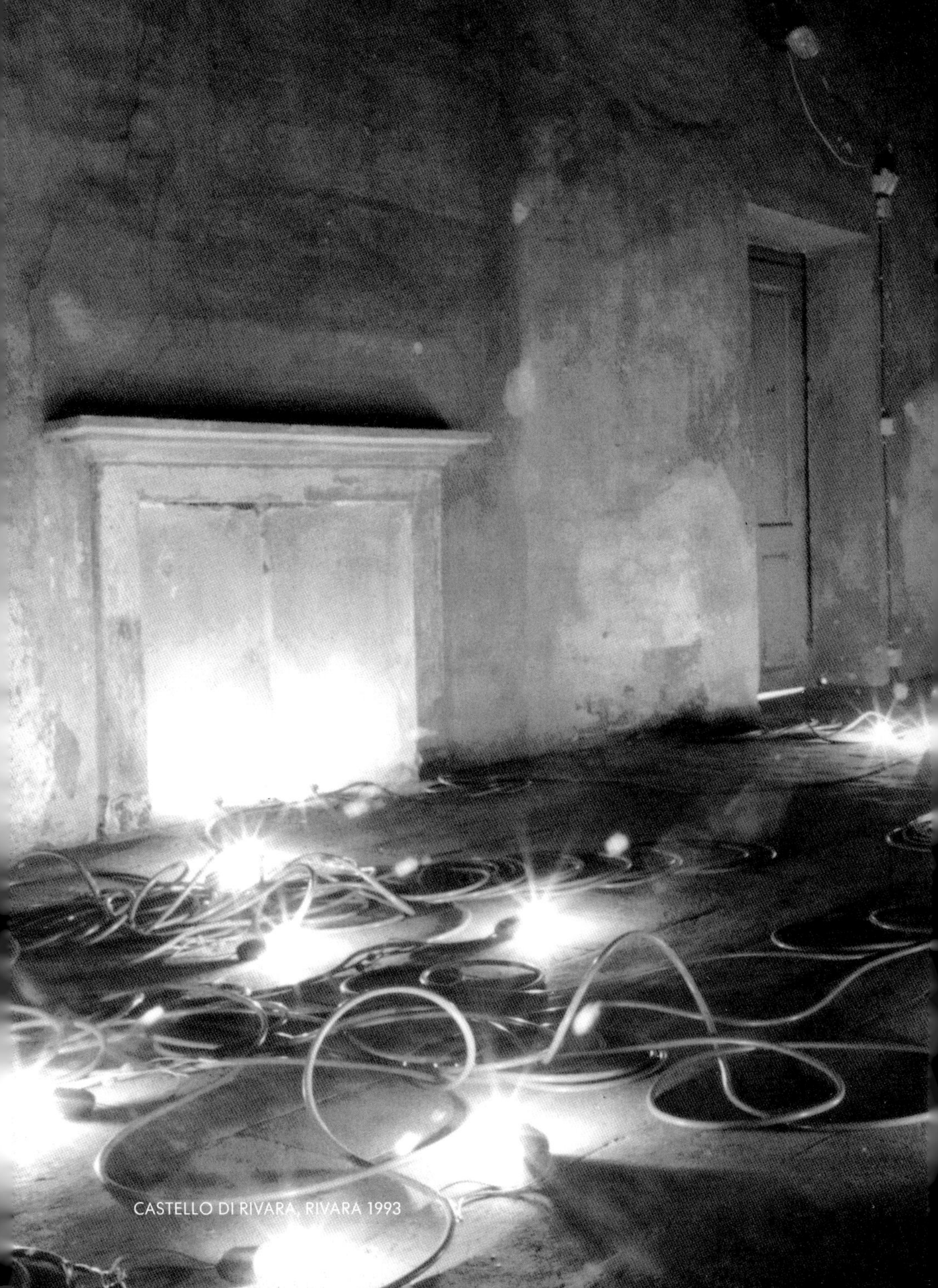
CASTELLO DI RIVARA, RIVARA 1993

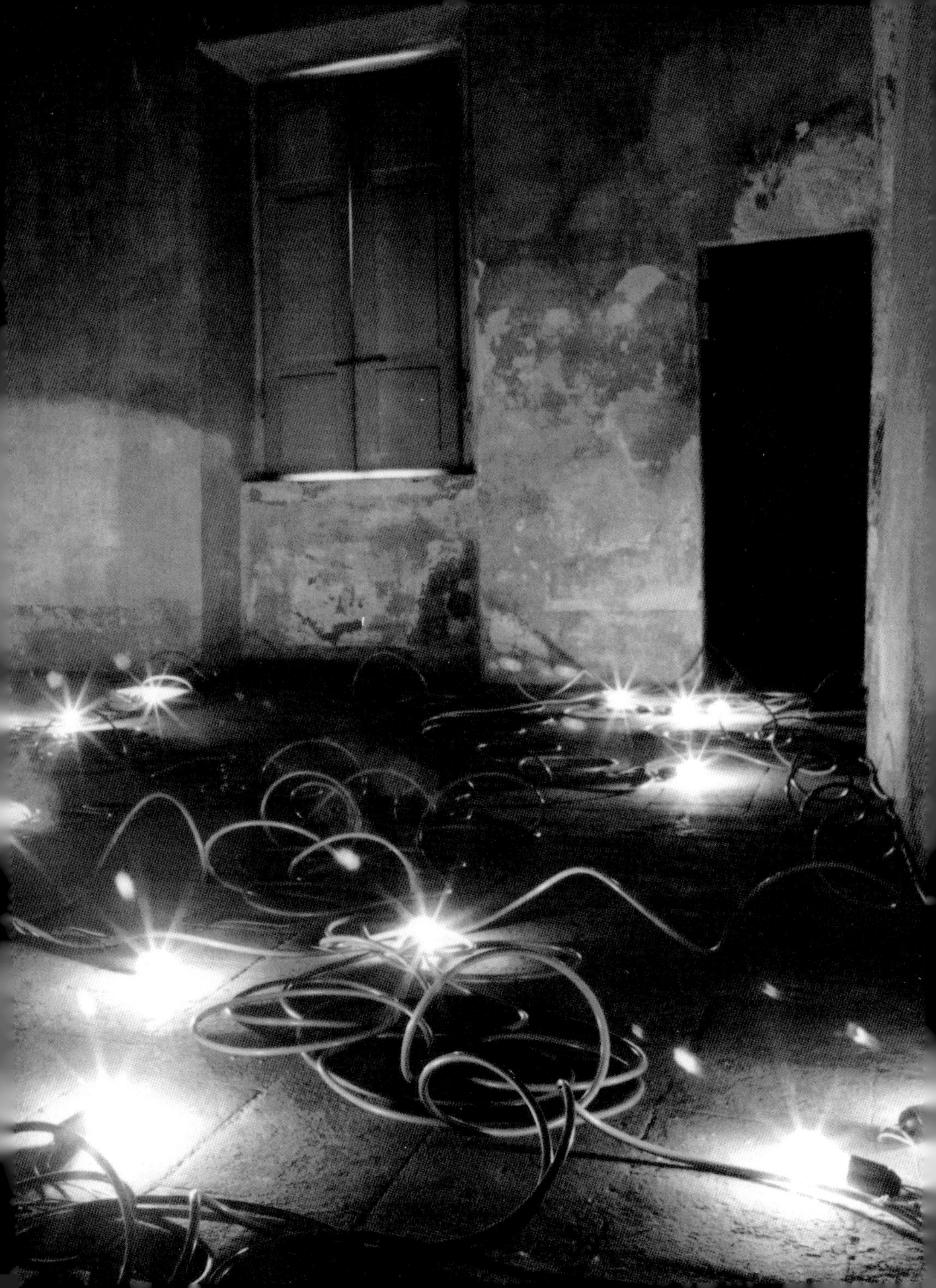

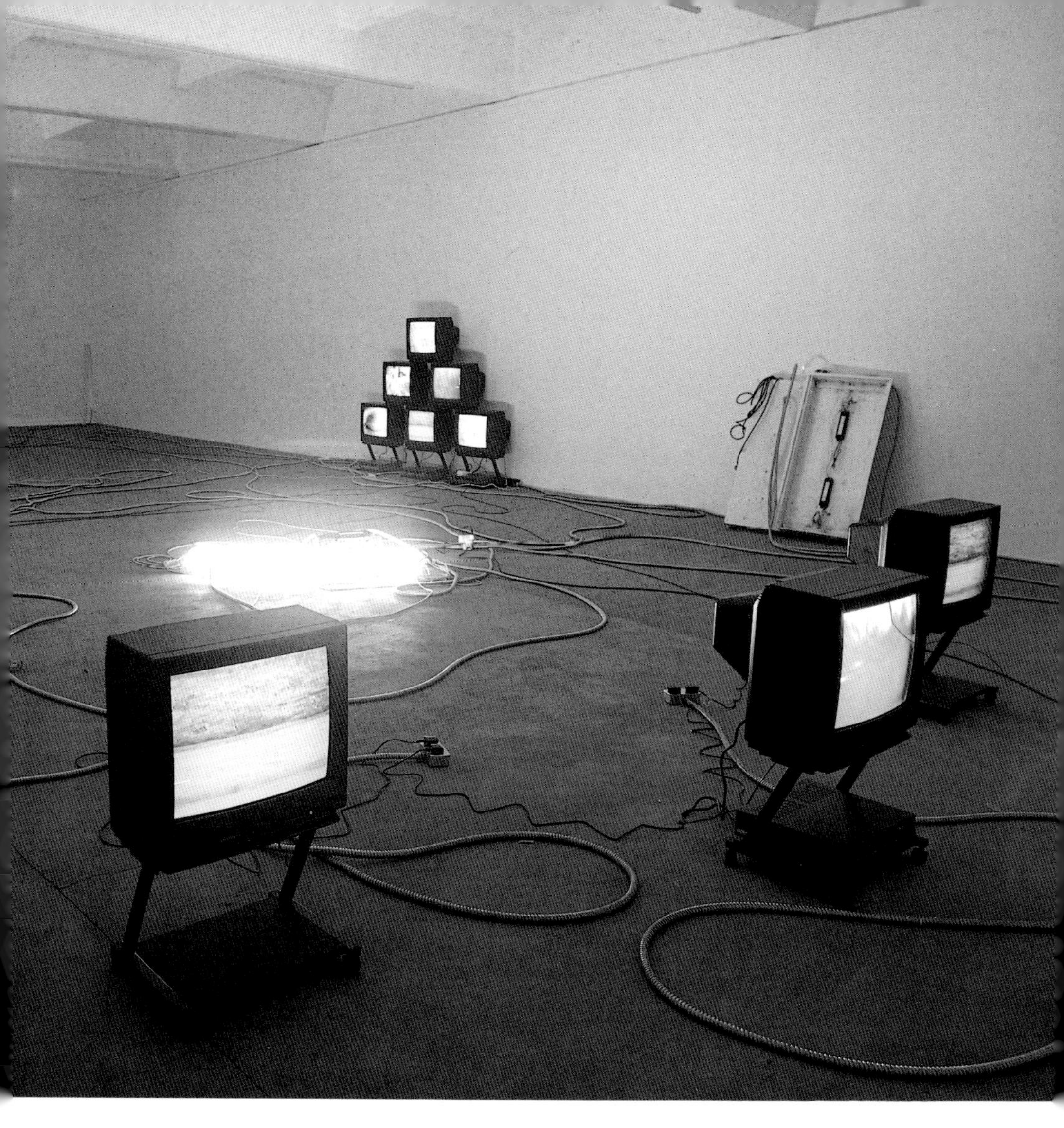

CHISENHALE GALLERY, LONDON 1993

The winding cables present themselves as *bowels*, as the building's inner life: an animistic view not without its own logical and more than metaphoric evidence if one considers that the data carried by the material cable conductor must be *digested*. The data might be *easily digested,* it might be *indigestible.* Yet the cabling and wiring also present metaphors for a data-keyed society which thinks in chips and megabytes and for which the computer has become the *net-work* preconditioning and guaranteeing functionality. Both consumption and, on an increasing scale, production are controlled by data flow. Artificial transmission and natural biological transmission are already thought of as compound units: bioenergetics, biophysics, biochemistry, gene technology, and "virtual reality" constitute the parameters. The latest construction strategies function biomimetically: airfoil construction is modelled after the microbiological structure of insect wings; wireless espionage communication and maritime echo-depth sounding imitate the perception systems of bats.

That the *artificial* and the *natural* are not destined to remain two distinct levels of reality has been obvious at least since biotronics, since the realization – first expressed in the literary genre of science fiction – that the man-machine interface represents a blurred border. Such scenarios, thought through, have radical consequences reaching far beyond the narrative presence: consequences for philosophy in general and epistomology in particular. That technology has magical qualities is also evident in the fact that we use it without reflection, merely as an instrument, a means to an end, almost unconsciously. Gearwheels, drive rods and V-belts all reveal how they work by virtue of their form and the forces they mobilize. In contrast, electricity cables, chips and digital meters do not tell the story of their technical conditions and processes. Nothing is actually visible or actually moving, yet energy is transmitted: an idea too complicated to comprehend from the viewpoint of mechanical logic.

McCaslin's installations refer to all of these inter-relations. His aesthetic cognitive achievement lies in presenting the remains, the artifacts, the "objets trouvés" of energy and information transmission within the coordinate system of mechanical logic. Hence form and function move contrarily or are at least out of alignment. The mode of expression in his installations questions unquestioning functionability in that he drives the functions ad absurdum; to paraphrase Francis Picabia: "The head is round to enable thoughts to change direction." In McCaslin's work, the technical (construction) remains of the cables, wires, grids

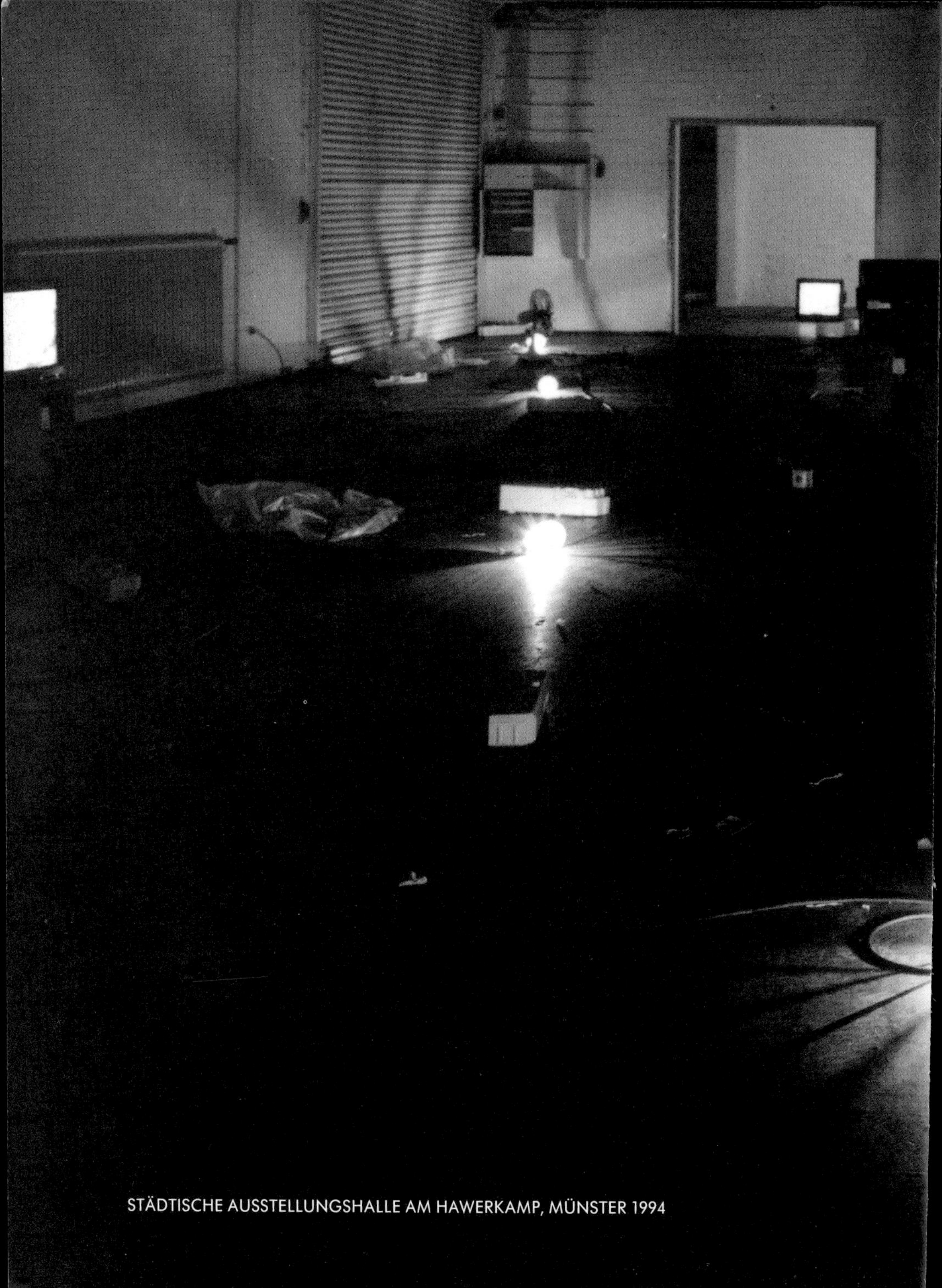

STÄDTISCHE AUSSTELLUNGSHALLE AM HAWERKAMP, MÜNSTER 1994

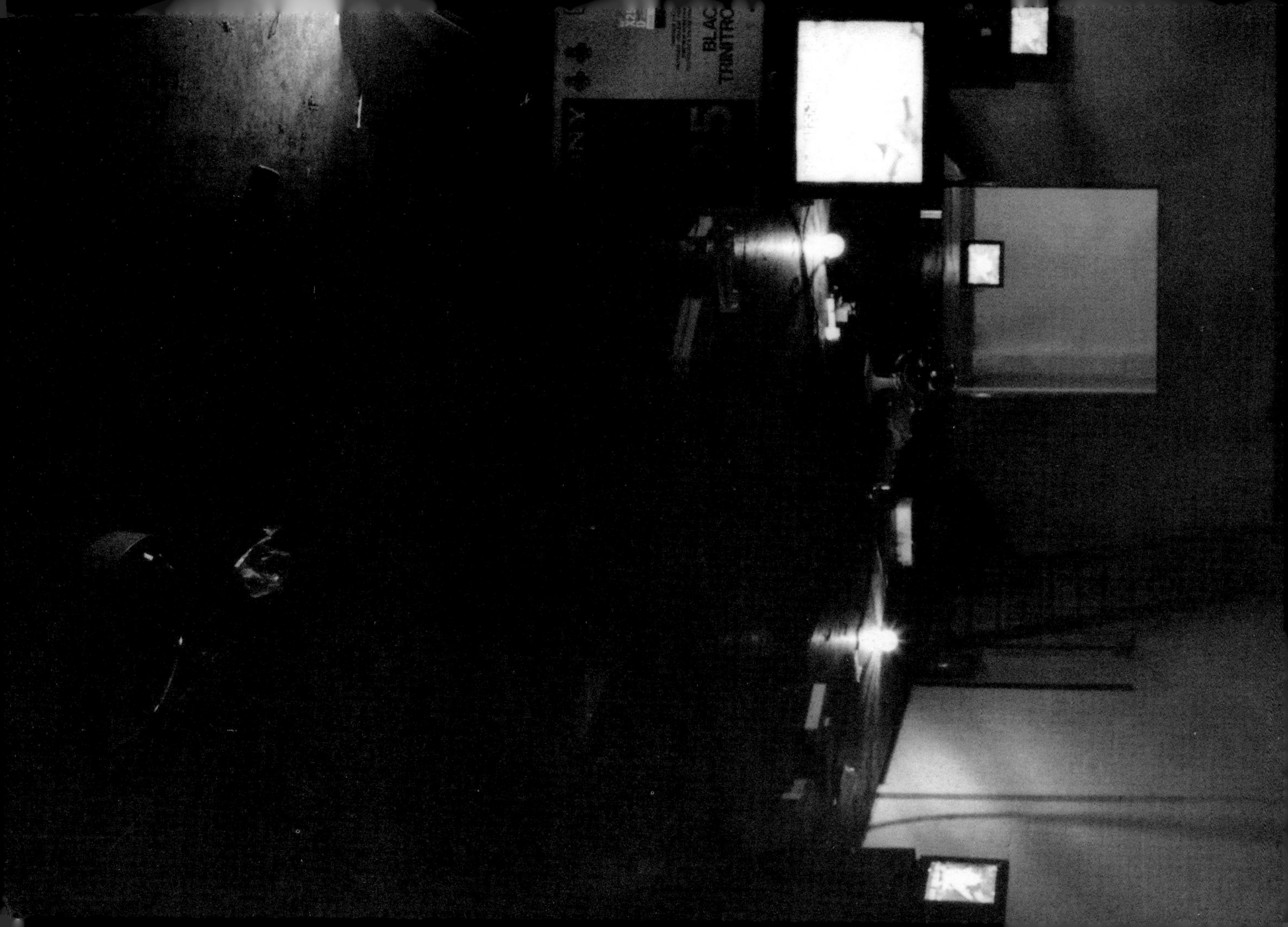

BLAC
TRINITRO
SONY

and switches become sur-real in the true sense of the word, for they evoke a magical function completely removed from their customary use. And as did the Surrealists, Matthew McCaslin endows his installations with metaphoric, magical titles such as "Fisheye Jungle," "See Spot Run" or "My Shoes Are Smiling." This last work is comprised of six ghetto-blasters standing on the floor, cabled together and bathed in a play of light and deep shadow by an oversized light bulb positioned between the radios. Here too we find the idea of the world as a "global village", consisting only of simultaneously generated data independent of locale, and the concept of a ghetto youth culture interested only in blaring noise loud enough to drive away thoughts of no future.

What flows through these cables – the energy, the sound, the information – is both material and immaterial. Currents of energy can be quantified and regulated. And these currents are increasingly becoming the regulatory system governing both world and society. In this sense, McCaslin's concern with energy currents amounts to the pragmatic American answer to the energy concept of someone like Joseph Beuys as exemplified in the "Honey Pump."

The quantification of the immaterial – or at least our desire to achieve it – is also emphasized by the clocking meters, those chronographs the artist so frequently and conspicuously integrates in his installations. Often cabled together and complemented by regulators, sockets or "technical units," they focus on our contemporary preoccupation with measuring time: a thousandth of a second makes the difference between a champion and a loser; the eight-hour-day is being redefined; we clock in at work; time bombs tick. Even the end of the world is usually referred to using a metaphor telling time, whether it be "five of twelve" or "five after twelve." That time passes irretrievably, that in a certain sense it *drips* away, was a theme the Surrealists took up. Yet it was not until accurate timekeeping was introduced that the "Modern Age" dawned, a modern era in social, technological, cultural and logical terms. The expressions "ration" and "irrational"[1] are closely related not only in an ethmyological sense. The rationality of the yardstick, the clock, the right angle – essential constituents of contemporary building technology – has become hyperrational, often bordering on hubris. McCaslin's wires and meters, his loudspeakers and light bulbs, thus can be interpreted as indicators of an expansion of our senses (or our sensuous-ness?) which may prove either good or bad. Electricity can be harnessed to produce heat – or used as a means of torture; light extends the day, but an excess can be light pollution; video and audio transmission enable us to take part in world events, be they classical concerts, bowing matches, a Himalayan expedition, or man on the moon. Yet pictures and sound can also infantilize us if they are inflationary and ubiquitous. We become incapable of distinguishing between fact and commentary, between our own and a parroted opinion; the truth is embellished, fictionalized. Recent surveys have shown that "reality TV," "info-tainment" and news programs are steadily gaining the quality of "background buzz." Everything under the sun can – and is – turned into "public relations."

Matthew McCaslin's installations refer to this level as well, particuarly because they dispense with the elaborate trappings of high-tech equipment so rampant in artistic installations of the so-called "New Media." On the contrary: they are stripped down to near-Calvinist sobriety. Only thus are they capable of compelling us to perceive and contemplate the "essentials" of a highly complex, artificially constituted world.

Simply because they refrain from telling a – complete – story, McCaslin's pieces own the clarity of haiku, that form of Japanese verse capable of condensing a complex thought into three lines of poetry. They are ontological frames for the perception of time and technology, at once both abstract and substantial.

Cloaked in an utter lack of deliberation, the works reveal a calculated intention laying claim to chaos while generating an inherent order. "The World on a Wire," to quote the title of a film from Fassbinder, gains a concrete yet almost mystical quality in McCaslin's installations. The diversity of meaning, a complex system of cross-associations, can be summarized in a single sentence by Guillaume Apollinaire: "The wise man laughs with a tremble." Proceeding from the energy currents that ultimately define entropy as the fundamental constant in the world and in life, Heraclitus deduced a basic law of reality: "panta rhei" – "everything flows."

Anna Meseure

Translated from the German by Mary Fran Gilbert

1 Translator's Note: The German here, not quite translatable, is "Messen" and "Vermessen." The word "messen" means "to measure"; the word "vermessen" to "mismeasure" in the broadest sense, i.e. to be audacious and daring (at the risk of miscalculating the outcome).

Matthew McCaslin

1957 in Bayshore, N.Y. geboren.
Lebt in New York.
Born 1957 in Bayshore, N.Y.
Lives in New York.

Einzelausstellungen | Solo Exhibitions

1987
Bess Cutler Gallery, New York

1989
Landscapes of the Inbetween,
Daniel Newburg Gallery, New York
(mit | with Steve di Benedetto)

1991
Daniel Newburg Gallery, New York
Le Consortium, Dijon
Feigen Inc., Chicago
Daniel Weinberg Gallery, Los Angeles
Anthony Reynolds Gallery, London
The Sky is Falling, Galerie Jennifer Flay, Paris

1992
Daniel Weinberg Gallery, Los Angeles
Tribute to a Moment, The Museum of Modern Art, New York
Art & Public, Genf
Galerie Rolf Ricke, Köln

1993
Event, Daniel Newburg Gallery, New York
Castello di Rivara, Rivara
Galerie Jürgen Becker, Hamburg
(mit | with Steve di Benedetto)
Chisenhale Gallery, London

1994
Städtische Ausstellungshalle Am Hawerkamp, Münster
Sprengel Museum Hannover

 Bibliographie (Auswahl) | Selected Bibliography

Gretchen Faust: Matthew McCaslin, in: Arts Magazine, Februar 1990
Roberta Smith: Matthew McCaslin, in: The New York Times, 6. Juli 1990
Elisabeth Hess: Caution: Artists Working, in: Village Voice, 18. Dezember 1990
Robert Mahoney: Matthew McCaslin, in: Arts Magazine, April 1991, S.104
Jan Avgikos: Matthew McCaslin, in: Artforum, Mai 1991, S.145
Saul Ostrow: Matthew McCaslin, in: Tema Celeste, Mai/Juni 1991, S.100
Eric de Bruyn: Matthew McCaslin, in: Artscribe, Sommer 1991, S.69
Paul Ardenne: Matthew McCaslin, in: Art Press, November 1991
Joshua Decter: Matthew McCaslin. Installations From On High, in: Flash Art, November/
Dezember 1991, S.127
Fereshteh Daftari: Matthew McCaslin, in: projects 33. Matthew McCaslin, The Museum of
Modern Art, New York 1992
Pascal Pique: McCaslin, in: Kanal Europe, April/Mai 1992, S.99/100
Holland Cotter: A builder's eye. Matthew McCaslin, in: The New York Times, 15. Mai 1992
Eric Troncy: Not Quiet, in: Art Press, Juni 1992
Gretchen Faust: Matthew McCaslin: »Event«, in: Forum International, Mai–August 1993,
S.144
Gretchen Faust: (Untitled), in: Matthew McCaslin, Chisenhale Gallery, London 1993

Der Band »Matthew McCaslin.
Ausstellungen – Exhibitions« erscheint
anläßlich der Ausstellungen des Künstlers
im Sprengel Museum Hannover 1. 3. – 30. 4. 1994
und in der Städtischen Ausstellungshalle
Am Hawerkamp, Münster 18. 2. – 3. 4. 1994.

Die Abbildungen wurden von den Galerien
und Ausstellungsinstituten zur Verfügung
gestellt.

Redaktion: Dietmar Elger

Gestaltung: Karin Girlatschek

Satz: Fotosatz Weyhing GmbH, Stuttgart

Litho: C + S Repro, Offset Reproduktionen GmbH,
70794 Filderstadt

Gesamtherstellung:
Dr. Cantz'sche Druckerei
Ostfildern bei Stuttgart

© 1994 Cantz Verlag und Autoren,
Abbildungen Matthew McCaslin

ISBN 3-89 322-270-7

Cantz Verlag
Senefelderstraße 9
73760 Ostfildern
Tel. 07 11 / 4 49 93 - 0
Fax 07 11 / 4 41 45 79

Printed in Germany